Two Tongues

New Women's Voices Series, 149

poems by

Lana Issam Ghannam

Finishing Line Press
Georgetown, Kentucky

Two Tongues

New Women's Voices Series, 149

Copyright © 2019 by Lana Issam Ghannam
ISBN 978-1-63534-950-4 First Edition
All rights reserved under International and Pan-American Copyright Conventions. No part of this book may be reproduced in any manner whatsoever without written permission from the publisher, except in the case of brief quotations embodied in critical articles and reviews.

ACKNOWLEDGMENTS

I'm grateful to the editors of the following publications in which these poems first appeared:

Common Ground Review: "When They Found Mohammed Abu Khieder" (forthcoming)
Harbinger Asylum: "America is a Ghost in Me"
Sinkhole: "Mama's Hijab is my Heirloom"
Orison Anthology: "there is a stillness after you"
Mudfish: "Mama's Hijab"
Prism Review: "If You Ask for my Hand" and "I'll Hear Him When the Trees Move"
Raleigh Review: "there is a stillness after you"
Mississippi Review: "Phases: Root, Blossom, Wing"
Spoon River Poetry Review: "Good Rest, Uncle" and "Names My Arab Mother Gives Me"
Sukoon: "Ebtesam, My Mother's Portrait" and "Two Tongues"

Publisher: Leah Maines
Editor: Christen Kincaid
Cover Art: Michael Colby
Author Photo: Lana Issam Ghannam
Cover Design: Elizabeth Maines McCleavy

Printed in the USA on acid-free paper.
Order online: www.finishinglinepress.com
also available on amazon.com

Author inquiries and mail orders:
Finishing Line Press
P. O. Box 1626
Georgetown, Kentucky 40324
U. S. A.

Table of Contents

America is a Ghost in Me 1

Ebtesam, My Mother's Portrait 2

Good Rest, Uncle 4

I am the Axis 5

If You Ask for my Hand 6

I'll Hear Him When the Trees Move 8

Mama's Hijab 9

Mama's Hijab is my Heirloom 11

Names my Arab Mother Gives Me 12

Phases: Root, Blossom, Wing 14

Theology of my First Rug 17

There is a stillness after you 18

When They Found Mohammed Abu Khieder 19

You Have Your Sedo's Eyes 20

Two Tongues 21

*For my sons, Adam and Rami—
so that you may know me through each part of my life.*

*For my family, especially my mother—
because these moments are your stories, too.*

America is a Ghost in Me

Lately I'm pulled up like roots above ground,
shaping days like broken mazes that lead me
from one road to the next, losing myself along the way.
But if I listen, I can hear the gunshots pointing north,
my country's compass on a map of shaken worlds. America
has been planted in my chest as a carnivorous seed
sprouting and wrapping its vines between my ribs.
Some days it holds my heart in its leaves and wipes away
the dirt that's settled. Then there are darker days
when the branches reach and thorn all of my muscle
and squeeze. On those days, I can't breathe.

My wrinkled soul feels lighter now, transparent as morning mist.
There was a time I could see it nestled on the crest
of each wave in my hair, under the nail of each finger.
Now, my woman-soul only comes out at night, a stolen ghost
of each body at the end of hot metal. These are the heaviest nights.
How do I fill myself up again? Where do I find the knife
whose tongues are sharp enough to cut my insides loose?
Give me the songs of each body pushed to the ground,
the furrowed brows of each face pushing against the weight,
if it means I can cut away the trees and let the light in again.

Ebtesam, My Mother's Portrait

Your eyes search for the star sewn
into the farthest corner of God's blanket

—its lacework woven with cancer
and sliding skin. Your spine is bent

under Baba's weight, the man who stole you
from the east. I look like you: teeth sitting

crooked, sharp, between lips plastered
down at the edges, but I crave your smile

with whimpers so brash I call them
laughter. You, with your hair wrapped

in scarves and pins to hide something
that marks beauty. You with your gorilla

paws for feet, cross-legged on the couch
like a lady-in-waiting. Waiting.

Is it a grave for your captor
that you seek? A bed of peace lined

with rocks and weeds, a plate over
his face to catch the drowning dirt—

this failing man who stole you
from the east? His heart, a beating drum

of a puppeteer who plays music so wild
my dancing hips can't hold its pace.

Baba can't hold it still. Your face wears
questions like body armor—unasked, undressed.

You're a woman routing your children
with cherub hands, your soul on fire

with the pages of a book creased
and spine bent. Like your back beneath

your lover's weight, the prince
who stole you from the flaming east.

Good Rest, Uncle

> *"Inna lillahi wa inna ilaihi raji'oon."*
> "To Him we belong and to Him we shall return."
> —Surah Al-Baqara 2:156

I climbed the fence that cradled your body in the ground—
softened by sprinklers that watered your sleeping skin—
beneath the brown and yellow grass, beneath the stone

that bears your final name (our name) that strung
your middle life with my beginning one. The links
jerked holes in my jeans when I mounted it between my legs.

Had I not tried for the other side, would you have felt
the glow of my sad eyes? Looking through to you
with only words too shy for the light? I heard my father speak

into cameras about hatred-heated gun barrels in gas stations,
like the one you worked at in the city. The owner bought the stone
with your final name on it, slipped off his guilt of your face broken

into pieces by a bullet. Had I not opened my hands to our sky
in hope to catch the falling goodness—*duaa* piling in the curves
of my palms to sprinkle like flowering seeds over your bed

in the damp dirt—had I not spoken the words, would you have felt
The Opening and your end, the first surah when you were born,
the last as you mold to the mud, missing parts from a grave;

you who wandered so long ago astray, *walad'daalleen…*

I am the Axis

Olive trees and *zam zam* water
live in me like garden spiders

that sleep in the leaves, and I teeter
to the east with dark cascades of waves

down my spine; long lashes sweep
my high cheeks. Then I fall back

to the western waves—a current
where both sides of the world meet

—the pull between two deserts
that have begun to drown together.

If You Ask for my Hand

this is no young lovers' tale
if you can't sniff

moonlight off my neck

without tongue lashes
from Mama's foreign mouth.

her voice designs sandstorms

that sing to open sky.
her words are wild—

streams that break dams,

dare her to move—
turn to fire in her mouth.

her scorn spills like oil

in the breeze. my face
spatters with slick

humility, the dark spots

burning. yearning,
i make up stories about you.

i use her oil on my canvas,

paint her portraits
of mouths and muscle—

all the men you will be—

and hide them in a cupboard.
we sing these tales as treaties,

if only to collect

our softly-ringing bells
in a single mason jar.

I'll Hear Him When the Trees Move

for my father

Lightning splits my sky today. Angry,
it points its crooked finger at me, demands
to know where Baba is. I say the ground has him,

lets him rest as long as he likes.
I wait for the wind to pass through,
to make leaves sing something close.

The trees sound like Baba.
They shake like he did when he danced,
his belly bouncing side to side.

Baba stared out dirty windows, waited for the breeze
to sleep. When the leaves touched the ground,
Baba sang how *Al shajar wala mat'harich.*

He'd only notice colors stuck around a bright sun.
He'd forget to look outside when it rained.
He'd forget the earth's feelings, how it soaked us

in its own sad stories. Stories of adolescence
when volcanoes scarred its face, twisters
that pulled up its high skirts of land.

Baba lost himself in the sky before finding himself
in the ground. The world would lay her head down,
and he'd remind us all that *The trees don't bother to move.*

Mama's Hijab

I watched
her dress
for work—

early mornings
emanated
coffee beans

and aroma
candles.
My eyes

followed her
hands—
they wrapped

colored scarves
around
her head,

pinned them
in place
just above

her right ear:
reds, yellows,
greens, oranges.

They lit
her olive face
like a flame.

She'd walk
out the front
door, eyes clear,

back straight—
a peacock
that stood,

each color
erect in her
unruffled

feathers—
a bird
I can never be.

Mama's Hijab is my Heirloom

a bird I can never be.

I've plucked Mama's feathers
to wear for my own, her hijab a crown of jewels
passed down to me in song.
The words wrap around me in feelings speaking
freedom, fabric that calls me home
in my own skin. But am I woman enough
to own my body, and yet
man enough to show it? My faith is anchored
in soft soil, feet planted deep
so I can't chase the sun as it skips across the sky.
I grow beneath the ground,
I grow beneath the ground, I grow beneath the ground
in this America of coloring seas.
The mud and dirt on my face and hands paint me
as I am of this earth, this flame,
this habitat of endangered whispers that are carried
on the wind. Seeds drifting,
petal to mouth to hearts of creatures still learning
to love. And I wear this crown.
As a woman. As a woman. I own the roots of this land.
And I am my mama's favorite bird.

Names My Arab Mother Gives Me

She calls me *Teresa*
after the Mother because I feed
stray cats in our backyard,

because I let my father curse me
after he blesses my hands

for helping his swollen feet
into socks. She says I'm a *hanooneh*,
that my words are gentle on alligator skin,

the same words that get turned
onto their backs with their short legs

in the air like roaches reaching
for the broom bristles that try
to stick them. I carry kisses

on both cheeks from strangers, lipstick
bruises, dimples not deep enough

to accessorize my olive face.
She calls me *nur ayunha*
though I dimmed that light

when it used to grow in the sharp
corners of her cocoa powder eyes.

If I could, I'd climb trees and jump
from the tops onto the moon, borrow
some shine and drip it like dew

to soften my mama's eyes.
I would dig for a little extra to keep

locked up in my dresser drawer—
leftover moonshine—the kind
that wets our tongues from the sky.

Then she'll call me a *raj'al*,
a woman-man that works herself

into the world instead of lying
beneath the weight of the sun, to bloom
like heavy honeysuckle grown

from the ground, with only the wind
to dance with her—her waltz missing

steps in her swoons—as the moon
dances, and often trembles,
with the high and low tides of summer.

Phases: Root, Blossom, Wing

I.

My parents lay between ripples of rage
in the absence of their roots. Algae and sinking

seaweed blanket egos higher than *al-Khalil*.
Their eyes move out of stone, hard and deep.

I watch Mama kiss sea salt off Baba's weathered lips,
flavor on top of nature on top of turn off the lights

before she can scratch out her face and ask
for a new one. Then he carves her out of wood

with a pair of safety scissors, her smile chopped
into sharp corners when she looks at me. Now,

wrinkles play board games around her eyes. Shadows
fill her cracks like foundation until the sun washes her

with orange and yellow creams the morning after.

II.

I find a blue blossom growing on my skin,
its leaves an itch I can't reach. The blooms

peel away as I bathe my floral breasts.
I glow red, my cheeks like stuck rose petals.

I rock on pillows—pale. Dreams heave onto the floor.
Police sirens and trains coo me to sleep. I imagine

people behind me propped on walls like paintings—
like Mama's wide eyes the first time I say *fuck*,

while Baba snores against the breeze through the open window.
I scratch out their faces, ask for new ones—something different

to decorate my shrunken halls. God's pencil breaks
before He can finish—my parents now old smudges

on paper—His sharpener lost in Michelangelo's drawer.

III.

I fly naked into shame, my spine slipping out
when I get stuck at the window. I am the bandit

keeping Mama's heart in plastic Tupperware, Baba's mind
in pieces tucked in a box towards the back of my closet.

I press my face to the mesh screen, beaten, printed,
until I scratch it out to ask for something else, curled in a spineless

cocoon. I am painted wings. My face falls into seasons,
into reasons for wearing wings as armor, an identity lost

to my beetle brothers, *flitter, flit.* I chain their lives shut
so Mama can't feel words, Baba can't think them,

until I go far enough away to bring back their world
on a paper plate, coated with sugar, softened with sweet berries,

their hunger sated by my hands, fingers licked clean.

Theology of my First Rug

This *sijjad* that cradles my head,
this bridge to other worlds and other
lives and other skies, weaves its colors

together like rivers of words. Each drop
is a beg, is an ask, is a *why, please, now,*

and the river flows from inside my chest
to rise up and flood the clouds. *Don't forget
me, because I promise I haven't forgotten you.*

I lay my forehead over the soft fabric in *sujood*
and each time—and each guided time—is a sureness

that I will die. And I will die. I see my son
in the *sijjad* like I see my grandfather, only
my son still belongs to this world. I ask

to belong to this world for as long as I can,
and I hold my son's face in the dark

that is between my eyes and the floor.
If I should die, let it be here where my face
is buried in the *sijjad's* strongest current.

There is a stillness after you

> "*Inna lillahi wa inna ilaihi raji'oon.*"
> "To Him we belong and to Him we shall return."
> —Surah Al-Baqara 2:156

as if the moon stopped the pull of waves
to shore—the sand slips, the air asleep.

In this life, you were the core, the pit
of heat that kept us warm, where ashes

flicked in us deep. That morning, our brothers
and sisters prayed to the east with sweets

and pastries awaiting their mouths. Their fasts
were fasted and *duaa* demanded as your stillness

spread over us like a fog. Our bodies—the carriers
of old worlds—and eyes could only hold the sky.

Your stillness filled our pores with chants
and blessings—*kul sana wa inta salem*:

may every year now find you in new peace.
It's the elder soul you lifted to angels

before the world could close its large doors,
slipped like a whisper from your fingertips

with words that sang to home—
"*ahlan wa sahlan, ahlan wa sahlan*"

as your open arms calmed our shaken bodies,
"you are most welcome, you are most welcome."

When They Found Mohammed Abu Khieder

> *I know not with what weapons World War III will be fought,*
> *but World War IV will be fought with sticks and stones.*
> —*Albert Einstein*

They found his body burned with holes
that emptied his young insides. Sixteen,

though burnt skin aged his name.

Charred from flames that choked him
with dancing fingers, the people prayed.

It wasn't the fire's fault.

But I thought, how did the forest
not build the blaze? Weeds, vines, wood?

How did its red-soaked leaves

not get stuck in its hate, his smoking skin?
Jerusalem's trees grew too tall, raced

for hazy sky, when his body entered at *fajr*.

People saw him dragged into the car, searched
the broken ground, calling *Mohammed*, prophet-like,

as if they follow him now to war.

You Have Your Sedo's Eyes

> *One had loved and she had forgotten things. One had lived in a room and loved nothing.*
> —Charles Fort, "One Had Lived in a Room and Loved Nothing"

If I forget, could you forgive me
for my holding eyes? They're only
trying to search you for a name,
some label or signal of love
that I maybe used to feel. I think
about your *sedo's* eyes, and how
they looked at me with a wideness
and stillness that I felt, like a wilderness
air. He looked at me hard, trying
to remember my name beneath
the olive trees, my soul first sung
with *at-Tur* before your *sedo*
met your *teta* and made me
your mother. Your *sedo* forgot
my role in his glass world
that fell off the counter
and shattered on the linoleum
floor. In those days, I watched
as white coats walked over
the pieces, shards crunching
beneath their feet like seashells
on the pavement. In those days,
he breathed in a room that he
was leaving. He slept in a cloud
that he was dreaming. On that last
day, the day before his eyes
stayed shut, he looked up at me
and said my name. I share your *sedo's*
mind. He gave you your eyes.
If I forget, could you write your name
in my hand? Could you
draw your face on my eyes?

Two Tongues

Yesterday I didn't understand
a word—Arabic sounds crackled
in my ears like foil in a microwave.

Its letters wet
with rounded lips,

accented with Mama's native breath.
Rubbed raw by ancestors reclaiming
their skin, my identity shook

when I felt my name
could be replaced.

Cultured seeds had been caught
on foreign wind, spread over new land
and waters. American air soaked

my cautious lungs,
like breathing forgotten sounds

was illegal in this place. Mama translated
palpable Palestinian tongue
into English. My split mouth knew

the taste
of each vernacular spice,

flavors coating the ridges of my teeth.
She paused to ask if I finally understood,
but I had burned both tongues.

Additional Acknowledgments

Many thanks to Terry Ann Thaxton for reading and rereading these pieces until they all fit together.

Special mention of my husband, Stewart, who so often is the first to read my early drafts.

Loving appreciation to my brother, Yazen, and sister-in-law, Dominique, for their constant support in life and in words.

A heartfelt thanks to my sisters, Tanya and Lara, for celebrating each published piece with me in the middle of the night, and with the sincerest enthusiasm.

Lana Issam Ghannam's poetry has been nominated for the Orison Anthology Award in Poetry (2016), was a finalist for the New Letters Prize in Poetry (2015), and a finalist for the Mississippi Review Poetry Prize (2015). Her writing attempts to bring awareness to her bicultural upbringing, as well establish an understanding of her Middle-Eastern identity to those willing to learn about the way others live. Her poetry and prose have been published in journals, online and in print, such as *Sinkhole, Mississippi Review, Prism Review, Raleigh Review, Spoon River Poetry Review, Sukoon,* and *The Cape Rock*, among other journals. She is currently working on a full-length collection of poetry and lives in Florida with her husband and two sons.

www.ingramcontent.com/pod-product-compliance
Lightning Source LLC
LaVergne TN
LVHW041523070426
835507LV00012B/1770